I love reading

Really Big Dinosaurs
and Other Giants
by Monica Hughes

Consultant: Luis M. Chiappe, Ph.D.
Director of the Dinosaur Institute
Natural History Museum of Los Angeles County

BEARPORT
PUBLISHING

NEW YORK, NEW YORK

Credits

Cover, Title Page, 4, 6–7, 12–13, 24: Lisa Alderson; 5T, 14–15, 20–21, 22B, 23B: Luis Rey; 5B, 18–19, 22T, 23T: Shutterstock; 8–9: Ticktock Media Archive; 10–11: Simon Mendez; 16–17: Bob Nicholls.

Every effort has been made by ticktock Entertainment Ltd. to trace copyright holders. We apologize in advance for any omissions. We would be pleased to insert the appropriate acknowledgments in any subsequent edition of this publication.

Library of Congress Cataloging-in-Publication Data

Hughes, Monica.
  Really big dinosaurs and other giants / by Monica Hughes.
      p. cm. — (I love reading. Dino world!)
  Includes bibliographical references and index.
  ISBN-13: 978-1-59716-543-3 (library binding)
  ISBN-10: 1-59716-543-3 (library binding)
  1. Dinosaurs—Juvenile literature. I. Title.

QE861.5.H845 2008
567.9—dc22
                              2007017959

For more information, write to Bearport Publishing Company, Inc., 101 Fifth Avenue, Suite 6R, New York, New York 10003. Printed in the United States of America.

10 9 8 7 6 5 4 3 2 1

Contents

Really big!

Long ago, huge dinosaurs lived on land.

Other big animals lived at the same time.

Some of them flew through the air.

Others swam in the sea.

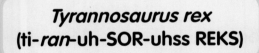

Tyrannosaurus rex
(ti-*ran*-uh-SOR-uhss REKS)

Quetzalcoatlus
(*kwet*-zal-koh-AHT-lus)

Elasmosaurus
(eh-*lazz*-moh-SOR-uhss)

5

A big meat-eater

Giganotosaurus may have been the biggest meat-eating dinosaur.

It was 49 feet (15 m) long from its nose to its tail.

It was as long as two dump trucks!

Giganotosaurus
(jig-ah-*not*-oh-SOR-uhss)

7

A super strong meat-eater

Tyrannosaurus rex may have been the strongest meat-eater.

It had powerful jaws.

T. rex could eat up to 500 pounds (227 kg) of meat and bones in one bite!

Tyrannosaurus rex
(ti-*ran*-uh-SOR-uhss REKS)

The heaviest plant-eater

Argentinosaurus was the heaviest plant-eating dinosaur.

It weighed 50 tons (45 metric tons).

A group of 14 elephants weighs about the same amount.

Argentinosaurus probably ate a kind of pine tree.

Argentinosaurus
(*ar*-jen-*tee*-nuh-SOR-uhss)

The tallest plant-eater

Sauroposeidon was the tallest plant-eating dinosaur.

It was 60 feet (18 m) tall.

That's as high as a six-story building.

Each bone in its neck was 4 feet (1.2 m) long.

Sauroposeidon was shaped like a giraffe, but was 30 times larger.

Sauroposeidon
(*sor*-uh-puh-SYE-don)

The biggest animal in the air

Quetzalcoatlus was the size of a small airplane.

It was not a dinosaur, but a flying **reptile**.

Its **wingspan** was about 40 feet (12 m) wide.

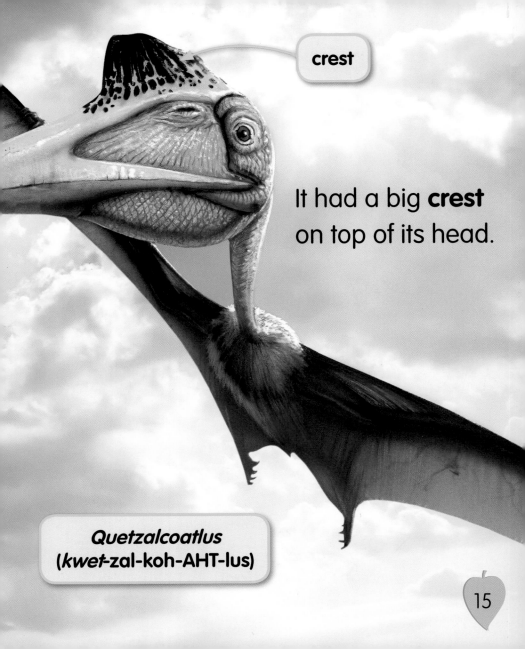

crest

It had a big **crest** on top of its head.

Quetzalcoatlus
(*kwet*-zal-koh-AHT-lus)

15

The biggest sea creature

Liopleurodon could weigh 100 tons (91 metric tons).

It was as heavy as 20 *Tyrannosaurus rex*!

It was not a dinosaur.

It was a reptile that swam.

Liopleurodon
(*lye*-oh-PLOOR-oh-don)

Its mouth was as long
as a large surfboard.

A long sea creature

Elasmosaurus was not a dinosaur.

This sea **creature** was 46 feet (14 m) long.

It was almost as long as a big swimming pool.

Its neck had as many as 75 bones in it.

A person's neck has only seven bones.

Elasmosaurus
(eh-*lazz*-moh-SOR-uhss)

19

A super big croc

Deinosuchus was a crocodile.

It lived during the time of the dinosaurs.

It may have been up to 48 feet (15 m) long!

That's longer than a school bus.

It was so big it could eat a dinosaur!

Deinosuchus
(*dye*-noh-SOO-kuhss)

Glossary

creature (KREE-chur)
an animal

crest (KREST)
an extra piece of
skin on top of an
animal's head

reptile (REP-tile)
a cold-blooded animal
such as a lizard, snake,
or crocodile

wingspan (WING-span)
the distance from one wing
tip to the other when
the wings are
spread wide

23

Index

Read More

Parker, Steve. *100 Things You Should Know About Dinosaurs.* New York: Barnes & Noble Books (2004).

Zimmerman, Howard. *Dinosaurs!* New York: Simon & Schuster (2000).

Learn More Online

To learn more about the world of dinosaurs, visit
www.bearportpublishing.com/ILoveReading